# The Teddy Bear Kit

### Alicia Merrett

HEADLINE

A QUARTO BOOK

Copyright © 1994 Quarto Publishing plc
First published in Great Britain in 1994
by HEADLINE BOOK PUBLISHING

All rights reserved. No part of this publication may be reproduced, stored in a retrieval system, or transmitted, in any form or by any means, without the prior permission in writing of the publisher, nor be otherwise circulated in any form of binding or cover other than that in which it is published and without a similar condition being imposed on the subsequent purchaser.

HEADLINE BOOK PUBLISHING
A division of Hodder Headline PLC
338 Euston Road, London, NW1 3BH

British Library Cataloguing in Publication Data

Merrett, Alicia
Teddy Bear Kit
I. Title
745.592

ISBN 0-7472-1086-1

This book was designed and produced by
Quarto Publishing plc, The Old Brewery, 6 Blundell Street, London N7 9BH

**Designer** Nick Clark • **Senior editor** Kate Kirby • **Editor** Janet Slingsby • **Senior art editor** Amanda Bakhtiar • **Photographer** Martin Norris • **Illustrations** Vana Haggerty, Elsa Godfrey (Patterns) • **Picture manager** Giulia Hetherington • **Art director** Moira Clinch • **Editorial director** Sophie Collins

Any statements, information and advice given here are believed to be true and accurate. However, neither the author, copyright holder nor the publisher can accept any legal liability for errors or omissions. The Publisher reserves the right to change the content of the kit without prior warning.

Special thanks to Margaret and Gerry Grey's Teddy Shop and to Roy Pilkington of Oakley Fabrics.

Typeset by West End Studios, Eastbourne.
Teddy bear components supplied by Winner Offset Printing Factory Ltd, Hong Kong.
Manufactured in Singapore by Eray-scan.

# Contents

### 4 • Bear in mind
Before you begin...an introduction to the book

### 5 • Bear faced
Creating facial features

### 6 • The bear necessities
Equipment and tools • Fur • Paw and pad fabric • Fillings
Joints • Threads • Stitches

### 8 • Bear bits
Eyes • Mouths and noses • Safety first

### 10 • Baby Bear
12 • Preparing the pattern  14 • Cutting out  16 • Pinning the pieces
17 • Sewing the pieces  18 • Joining the pieces  19 • Sew and turn
20 • Creating the features  22 • Jointing and finishing

### 24 • Mummy Bear
26 • Preparing the pattern  28 • Pinning and sewing  29 • Joining the pieces
30 • Eyes, nose and mouth  31 • Jointing and finishing

### 32 • Daddy Bear
34 • Preparing the pattern  36 • Pinning and sewing  37 • Joining the pieces
38 • Jointing and finishing

### 40 • Bear Wear
Patterns and instructions for making teddy bear clothes

### 46 • Bears! Bears! Bears!
A gallery of bears to inspire the bear-maker, plus useful contact addresses

# The bear facts

The Teddy Bear was born in 1903. Some claim it was invented in the United States, others say it was created in Germany. Wherever the place, it is widely agreed that the classic Teddy Bear – a furry, standing bear with an appealing face and a movable neck and limbs – appeared around that time in the toyshops of both the United States and Germany. Morris and Rose Mitchom claim the credit for inventing the "American" Teddy Bear. Their toy was based on a bear cub that President Theodore Roosevelt refused to shoot while trying to settle a border dispute in November 1902. The bear cub appeared in a famous political cartoon by Clifford Berryman, captioned "Drawing the line in Mississippi". This small bear became Berryman's signature on all his Roosevelt cartoons.

The Mitchoms made and quickly sold some toy bears at the time of the incident. They are said to have written to the President (whose nickname was Teddy) for permission to use his name for the bear. The Mitchoms went on to found the *Ideal Toy Corporation*, which was at one time the largest bear factory in the United States.

A restored pre 1910 Steiff bear.

About the same time, in Germany, Margarete Steiff, a wheel-chair bound toymaker and designer, made jointed bears based on her nephew's drawings of bears at the Stuttgart Zoo. They were offered for sale at the Leipzig Fair in 1903, and an American buyer ordered several thousand. The firm of Steiff grew and prospered, and still produces beautiful toys today.

In England, from 1909, the name "Teddy" (nickname for Edward) for a bear, spread widely under the reign of King Edward VII.

Whatever the truth, there is no doubt that the Teddy Bear is one of the most popular toys ever. Teddies are loved by children the world over, and are also collectors' items.

Two well-loved teddy bears.

# Bear in mind

4 • Introduction

Baby Bear
27cm (10½in)

Mummy Bear
35cm (14in)

Daddy Bear
40cm (16in)

**All dressed up** Bears can go bare or you can dress them up in Sunday best. Full instructions and patterns are supplied on pages 40-45.

In this book you will find patterns for making three different size bears: small, medium and large. The kit has all you need to make the small, "Baby" bear, which has been carefully designed to appeal to, and be safe for, children. In following the simple instructions step-by-step to make your **Baby Bear**, you will learn all the basic bear-making skills and be ready to tackle the medium-sized "Mummy" bear and the sophisticated "Daddy" bear, with his traditional long snout and humped back.

You will be amazed how bears, all made from the same pattern, look completely different depending on your choice of fabric and accessories. Bears intended as children's toys should be made in non-flammable man-made fur, with plastic safety eyes, nose and joints. But make up any of these three patterns in luxurious long-pile mohair and you will create a collectors' bear – especially if you style it with glass eyes and an embroidered nose! Or try making up one of the bears in cloth for a very different but equally lovable look. The photographs in this book will give you lots of ideas. Embroidering claws, shaving the muzzle, making clothes or just adding a simple bow, can all add enormously to the individual appeal of that very special toy – a Teddy Bear you have made yourself.

# Bear faced

The positioning of the eyes, nose and mouth are crucial to the personality of your bear. As in all hunting animals, bears' eyes face forward. They should be placed next to the face seams. Lower and wider indicate a younger bear – higher and closer an older bear. Wild bears move their ears quite a lot, so there are a number of possible positions to copy for your Teddy: looking forward, looking sideways, curved. The ears in younger animals are placed lower, in older animals higher.

Mouths can be created with straight or curved stitches, pointing up or down, to give your bear a serious, sad, mischievous or happy expression.

Always experiment with the position of the facial features before making an irreversible decision!

**Bear expressions** benign, sad, cute, grumpy...the expression you give your bear is in your hands. The subtlest changes to the positioning of the ears, shape of the mouth and arrangement of the eyes serve to make every handmade teddy special. From left to right: thoughtful bear, serious bear, content bear.

# The bear necessities

## Equipment and tools

**Small, pointed scissors** • For cutting fur fabric.

**Sewing machine** • Only straight machine stitch is required – with machine needles size 14 (90) or 16 (100). (The bear can be stitched by hand using double strong thread and a very small backstitch, but it is not recommended.)

**Hand-sewing needles** • Embroidery needles, which have larger eyes, to use for tacking and (with strong thread) for closing openings • A curved needle for stitching the ears • Extra long needles (90mm or 120mm, 3½in or 5in) for stitching glass eyes.

**Awl or thick knitting needle** • This is for making holes in the fur fabric where the joints, eyes and nose will go.

**Stuffing tool** • Best such tool is a wooden stick or dowel with a tapered end, or a knitting needle.

**Soft pencil, ball-point pen or dressmakers' chalk** • For marking the patterns on the fabrics.

## Fur

<u>Man-made fur fabrics:</u> look for a dense pile and soft texture. Most have knitted backs (as in the kit).

<u>Mohair:</u> real wool fabrics. The pile can be of different lengths; some are straight and some curly ("distressed"), imitating the old-fashioned plush fabrics. Most have woven backs.

## Paw and pad fabric

<u>Velvets/Velveteens:</u> dress or upholstery qualities. Many fray; they must be handled with care. They can be stabilized by ironing a piece of interfacing on the back.

<u>Real leather:</u> gloving quality is very pliable and good for luxurious collectors' bears.

<u>Imitation suedes:</u> called sueded fabric, suedette, display suede, ultrasuede. Does not fray.

<u>Felt:</u> only use the extra thick, 100% wool felt obtainable from specialist bear suppliers. Ordinary felt is made of viscose and it is not strong enough.

# Introduction • 7

## Fillings

**Polyester:** all purpose, best when springy and bulky. Choose good quality stuffings.
**Woodwool:** for collectors' bears. If used, pack well. It makes embroidering the nose easier on a polyester-stuffed bear if a handful of woodwool is placed in the nose.
**Plastic pellets:** gives a bean-bag effect. For collectors' bears only.

## Joints

Joints hold the bear together and allow it to turn its head and limbs.

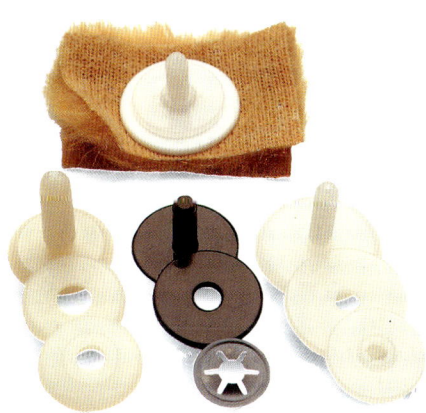

**Plastic joints:** these are safest and suitable for all bears. The shank joint goes inside the head or limb, with the shank protruding out though a hole. Another hole is made in the body and the shank slipped in through it. On the inside of the body, the washer is slipped onto the shank, and the plastic or metal fastener fitted to it firmly. The washer is the loose-fitting, disc-shaped component with the larger hole; the fastener has a comparatively smaller hole and fits tightly.

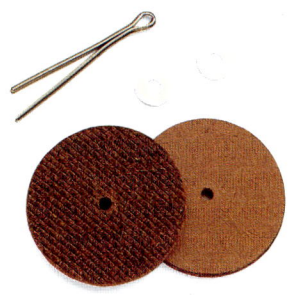

**Hardboard and split-pin joint:** this traditional type of joint can be used for collectors' bears. They are harder to fit and are composed of two hardboard discs, two very small metal washers and a metal split-pin which is bent into a "crown joint" to hold it together.

## Threads

For stitching the bears choose matching colour threads.
**Cotton or polyester or mixtures, size 50:** for machine sewing.
**Strong or buttonhole thread:** for closing openings.
**Embroidery thread, fine knitting wool, or darning wool:** in black or brown for embroidering noses.

## Stitches

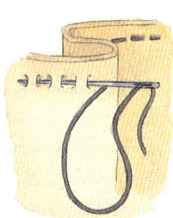

**Running stitch** Used for gathering and shirring fabric, running stitches are small and even. Take several stitches through the point of the needle before pulling it through the fabric.

**Tacking** Also known as basting, tacking holds fabric layers together temporarily. Using a contrasting thread, stitches should be between 5mm (¼in) and 1cm (⅜in) long.

**Ladder stitch** Used for invisibly closing openings. Similar to running stitch but with each stitch taken on the opposite side of the seam. To close, pull thread tight after two or three stitches.

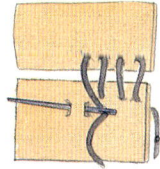

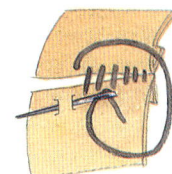

# Bear bits

## Eyes

**Noise-making devices can be fitted inside the tummy of bears.**
**Growlers** • These work by making a noise when the bear is tilted over. Good for larger bears.
**Squeakers** • These can be flat or concertina-shaped, and work by making a noise when pressed or squeezed; better for smaller bears.

grrrrrr!

Plastic safety eyes: suitable for all bears. The washer can be plastic or metal and it cannot be removed once fitted. These eyes have to be positioned before the head is stuffed.
Colours: black (imitating the old shoe-buttons), brown, blue, amber. They come in a range of sizes, from 9mm (⅜in) to 30mm (1¼in); most commonly used are 12, 14 and 16mm (½in, ⁹⁄₁₆in and ⅝in).

Glass eyes: these have wire loops, and are stitched in place after the head is stuffed. This allows a versatility in positioning that can make your bear more interesting. Glass eyes have a nice shine and look good on collectors' bears made with luxury fabrics.

Unfortunately they are much more expensive than plastic ones as, in many cases, they are hand-made. They come in sizes from 6mm (¼in) to 16mm (⅝in); colours are either black or a brown/amber/topaz colour. They are available from specialist bearmaking suppliers.

**Glass eyes are *not suitable* for children's bears because:**
- they can break and shatter
- they can be pulled out and swallowed.

## Mouths and noses

Mouths are always embroidered; use the same threads as for the nose. Various shapes are possible and they affect the personality of the bear.

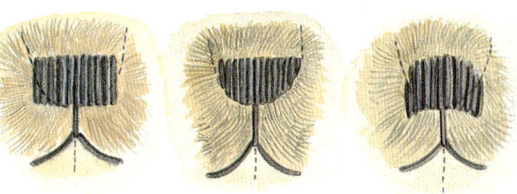

Traditional expression

Introduction • 9

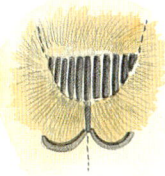  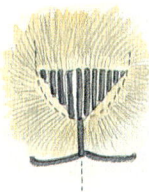

Happy expression

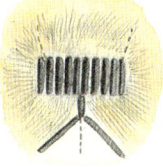  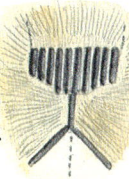

Serious expression

**Plastic safety noses:** suitable for all bears. They can be plain triangular or more realistic, with indented nostrils. All have plastic or metal washers, to hold them in place.

**Embroidered noses:** the traditional teddy bear nose; a must for collectors' bears. Various shapes are possible as the bear variations in this book show. Use black or brown perlé (thick)

embroidery thread, or fine knitting or darning wools. Securely sewn embroidered noses should be suitable both for children's and collectors' bears.

**Leather-covered plastic noses:** a triangular plastic nose can be covered with a small piece of pliable gloving leather, gathered and secured on the back. This gives a softer, warmer look to the bear.

## Safety first

When the first bears were made, there were few if any toy safety regulations, so things like swallowable shoe-button eyes, glass eyes on wires, flammable fabrics and stuffing materials, could all be used without constraints. Today, a toy bear meant for a child has to pass stringent safety tests, and therefore many "collectors' bears" may not be suitable for small children.

**To be suitable for children**
• Fabrics and stuffings have to be of low flammability, non-allergenic and non-toxic.
• Eyes and noses must not break easily, and have to be attached in such a way that they will not come off.
• Joints have to be firmly attached and non-rusting.
• All stitching in the bear has to be firm and well-anchored so that seams will not split open.
• Materials should be purchased from reputable dealers who can give reliable information as to their safety.
• If you are making bears to sell, check the regulations carefully beforehand.

**Supplied in your Baby Bear kit are the following items:**

**Man-made fur fabric with knitted back**
- 30cm × 50cm (12in × 20in)

**Suedette for paws and foot pads**
- 9cm × 12cm (3½in × 5in)

**Eyes**
- A pair, 12mm (½in) brown, plastic safety

**Nose**
- Triangular, 18mm (¾in) black, plastic safety

**Joints**
- five 30mm (1¼in) plastic safety

**Filling**
- 100g (4oz) polyester, good quality

**Thread**
- 1m (39in) embroidery thread for mouth

**Red ribbon**
- 1m (39in)

# Baby Bear

Ready, Teddy, sew! Everything you need to make a lovable and original bear is included in your kit. Your only problem will be deciding whether to keep **Baby Bear** or give him to a very lucky child!

Actual size

# Baby Bear

## Stage One
# Preparing the pattern

Trace or photocopy the Baby Bear pattern pieces shown full size. Look at the pattern pieces chart (right), and make (or photocopy again) as many duplicate pieces as are needed, turning pieces over to obtain a reversed "mirror image" pattern piece for those that require it. Transfer markings to the pattern pieces where necessary. For durability and ease of handling, glue paper pieces onto card and cut the card to the required shapes.

**From fur fabric**

**Ears**
- 4

**Head gusset**
- 1

**Head sides**
- 2, one reversed

**Body**
- 2, one reversed

**Inner arms**
- 2, one reversed

**Outer arms**
- 2, one reversed

**Legs**
- 2, one reversed

**From suedette**

**Foot pads**
- 2

**Paw pads**
- 2, one reversed

Seam allowances of 6mm (¼in) are included in the patterns

**HEAD GUSSET**
Cut one piece in fur fabric

Nose

Neck

**LEG**
Cut two pieces (one in reverse) in fur fabric

Leg joint

Leave open

Leave open for footpad

**EAR**
Cut four pieces

Leave open

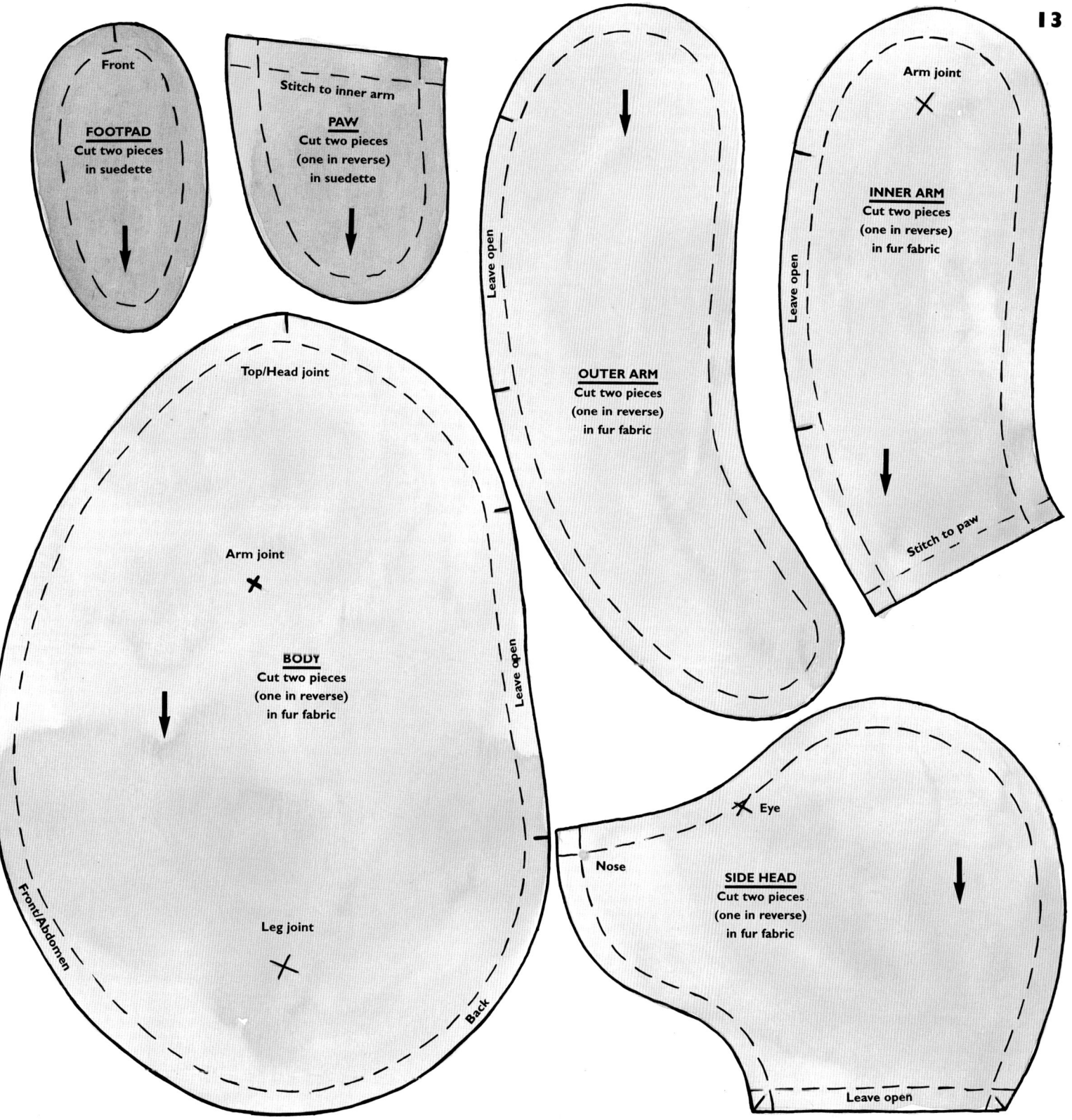

14  **Baby Bear**

# Stage Two
# Cutting out

The amount of fabric provided does not allow for errors. So make sure all the pattern pieces are in place in the positions shown in the photograph before starting to mark or cut. Use small pointed scissors to cut the fur.

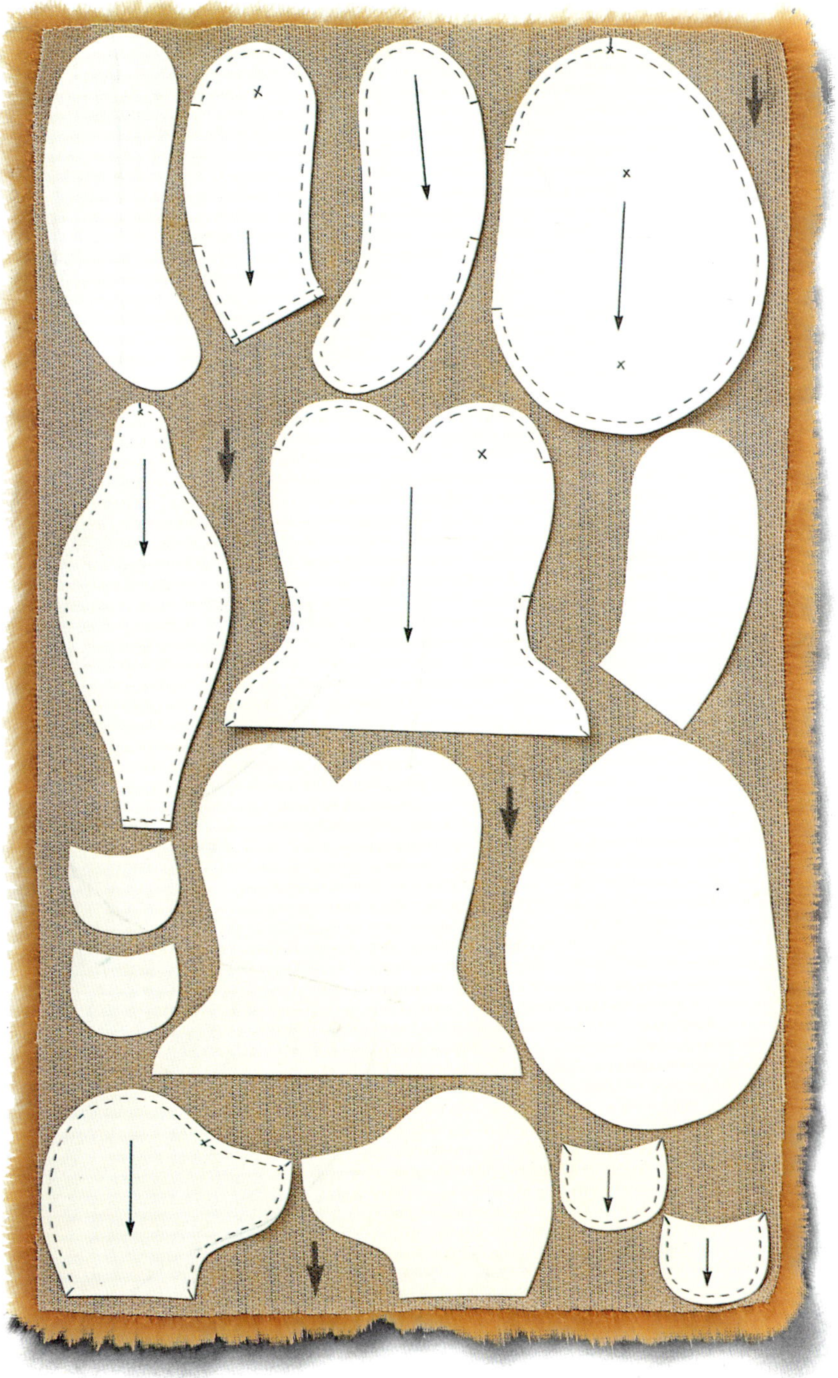

**🐾 1** Establish the direction of the pile of the fur fabric by stroking it, and mark the direction with arrows on the back. Place the card patterns, or pin the pattern pieces on the back of the fabric, the arrows in the pattern pieces pointing in the same direction as the arrows in the fabric, following the layout.

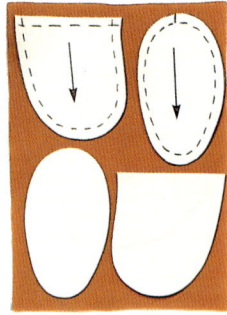

**🐾 2** Pin the foot pad and paw patterns on the back of the pad fabric, as shown.

**🐾 3** Mark round the fur and pad pieces with a soft pencil, a ball-point pen or dressmakers' chalk. Transfer to the fabric the markings for the placing of the eyes, nose, joints and openings. Remove the pattern pieces and pins (if used) and get ready to cut the fabric; slip the point of the scissors under the pile and snip the back of the fabric, pulling the pile apart as you go.

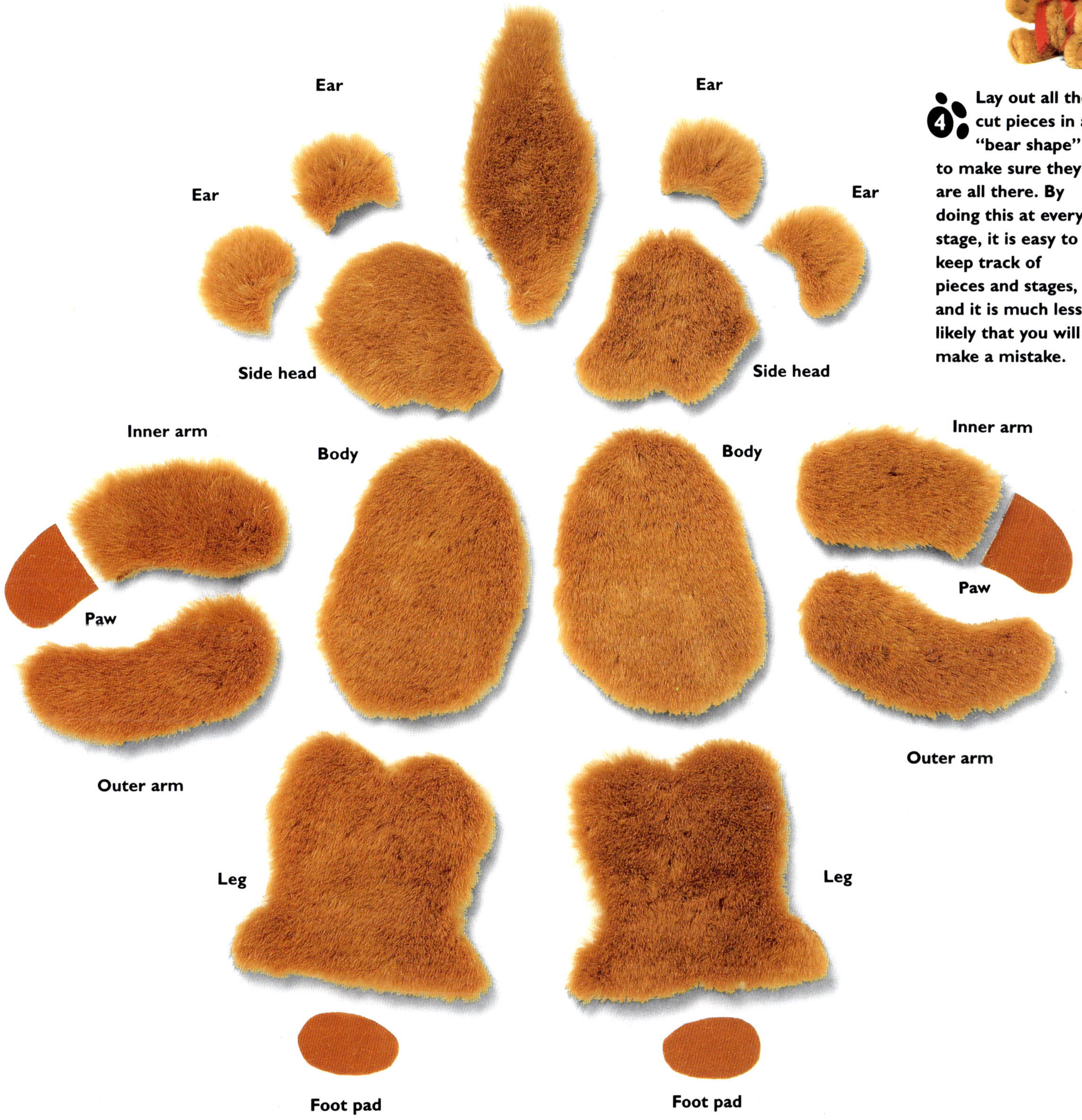

Head Gusset

Ear

Ear

Ear

Ear

Side head

Side head

**Baby Bear** 15

🐾 **4** Lay out all the cut pieces in a "bear shape" to make sure they are all there. By doing this at every stage, it is easy to keep track of pieces and stages, and it is much less likely that you will make a mistake.

Inner arm

Body

Body

Inner arm

Paw

Paw

Outer arm

Outer arm

Leg

Leg

Foot pad

Foot pad

# 16 Baby Bear

## Stage Three
# Pinning the pieces

Putting the right sides together, match and pin the pieces pushing the pile to the inside. In most cases, pins will be sufficient to hold the pieces while you machine them. Tacking is recommended for a few pieces.

**1.** Join the two side heads, right sides together. Pin from the nose to the neck only.

**2.** Pin the four ear pieces to make two ears, right sides together, along the long curved side only. Leave the short side open. (See detail, above.)

**5.** Pin the two body pieces, right sides together, leaving an opening in the centre back.

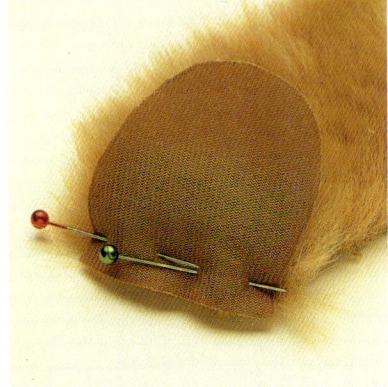

**4.** Pin the two suedette paws to the two inner arms, right sides together. (See detail, above.)

**3.** Fold over each leg, right sides together. Pin round from the top of the leg to the end of the toes, leaving an opening on the side as indicated. Leave sole area open as well to insert the foot pads later.

**Stage Four**
# Sewing the pieces

**Baby Bear** 17

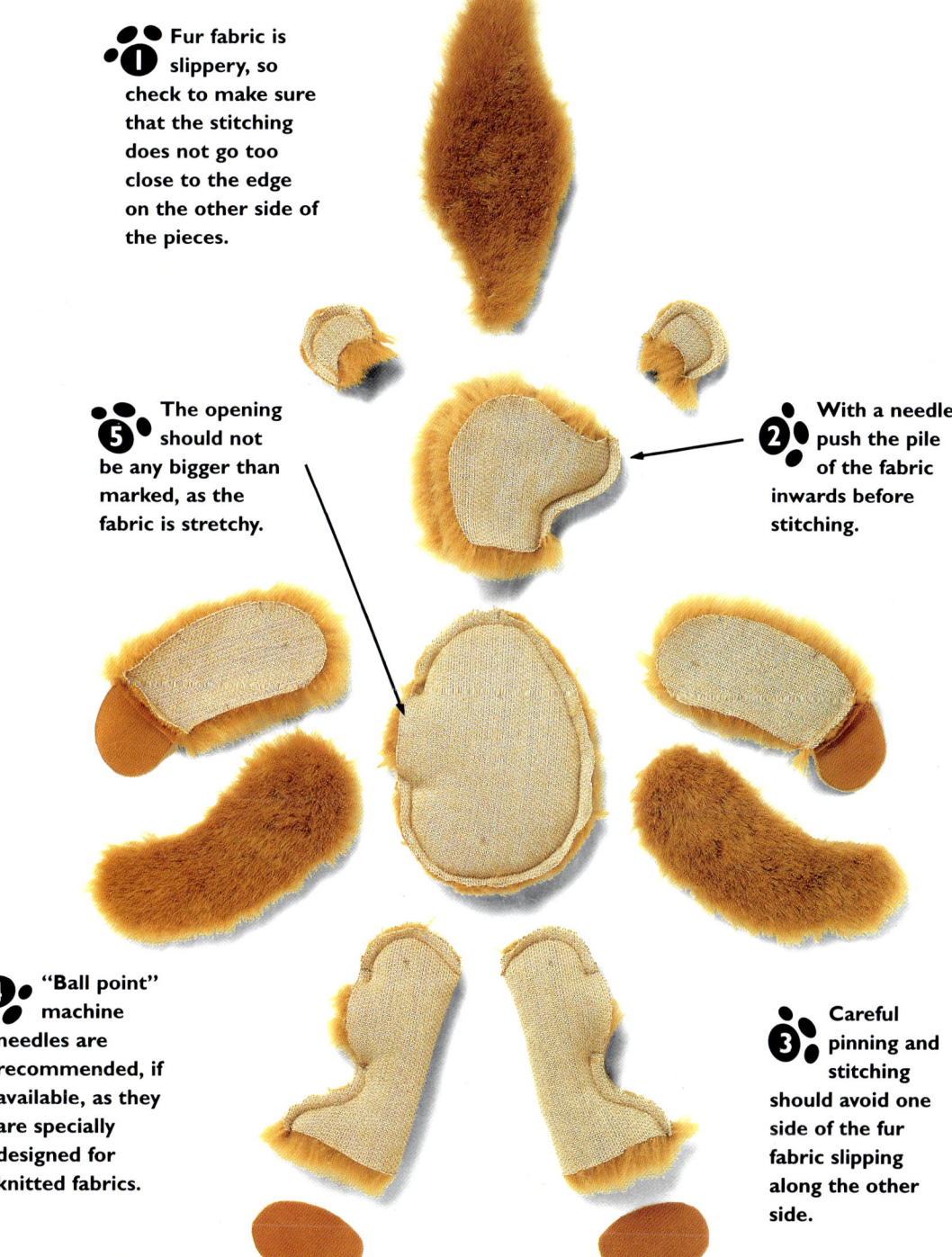

1. Fur fabric is slippery, so check to make sure that the stitching does not go too close to the edge on the other side of the pieces.

2. With a needle push the pile of the fabric inwards before stitching.

3. Careful pinning and stitching should avoid one side of the fur fabric slipping along the other side.

4. "Ball point" machine needles are recommended, if available, as they are specially designed for knitted fabrics.

5. The opening should not be any bigger than marked, as the fabric is stretchy.

Set your sewing machine to stitch the fur fabric, using needle size 14 (90) or 16 (100), and stitch size 2½. Test the stitching on scraps of the fur fabric before beginning to stitch the bear. Now machine stitch all the pinned pieces with a straight stitch, leaving a seam allowance of 6mm (¼in). Remove the pins as you sew.

# Baby Bear

## Stage Five
# Joining the pieces

**1.** Join the head gusset to the head sides. Start by pinning and tacking the nose end, and then work along each side towards the neck end, one side at a time. Tack these seams too, before machining. (See detail, left.)

**2.** The nose area can be hand-stitched if you find it difficult to machine stitch. Use double strong thread and a small back stitch.

**3.** Pin inner arms to outer arms, leaving an opening where indicated.

**4.** Pin foot pads to lower leg opening, matching front of pad with front seam. It is recommended that you tack this by hand before machining. (See detail, below.)

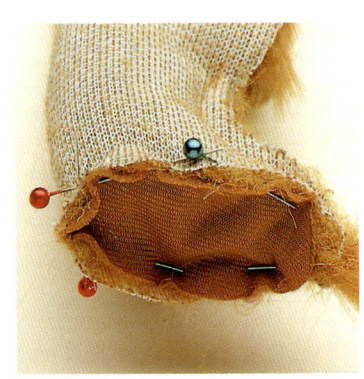

Stage Six
# Sew and turn

**Baby Bear** 19

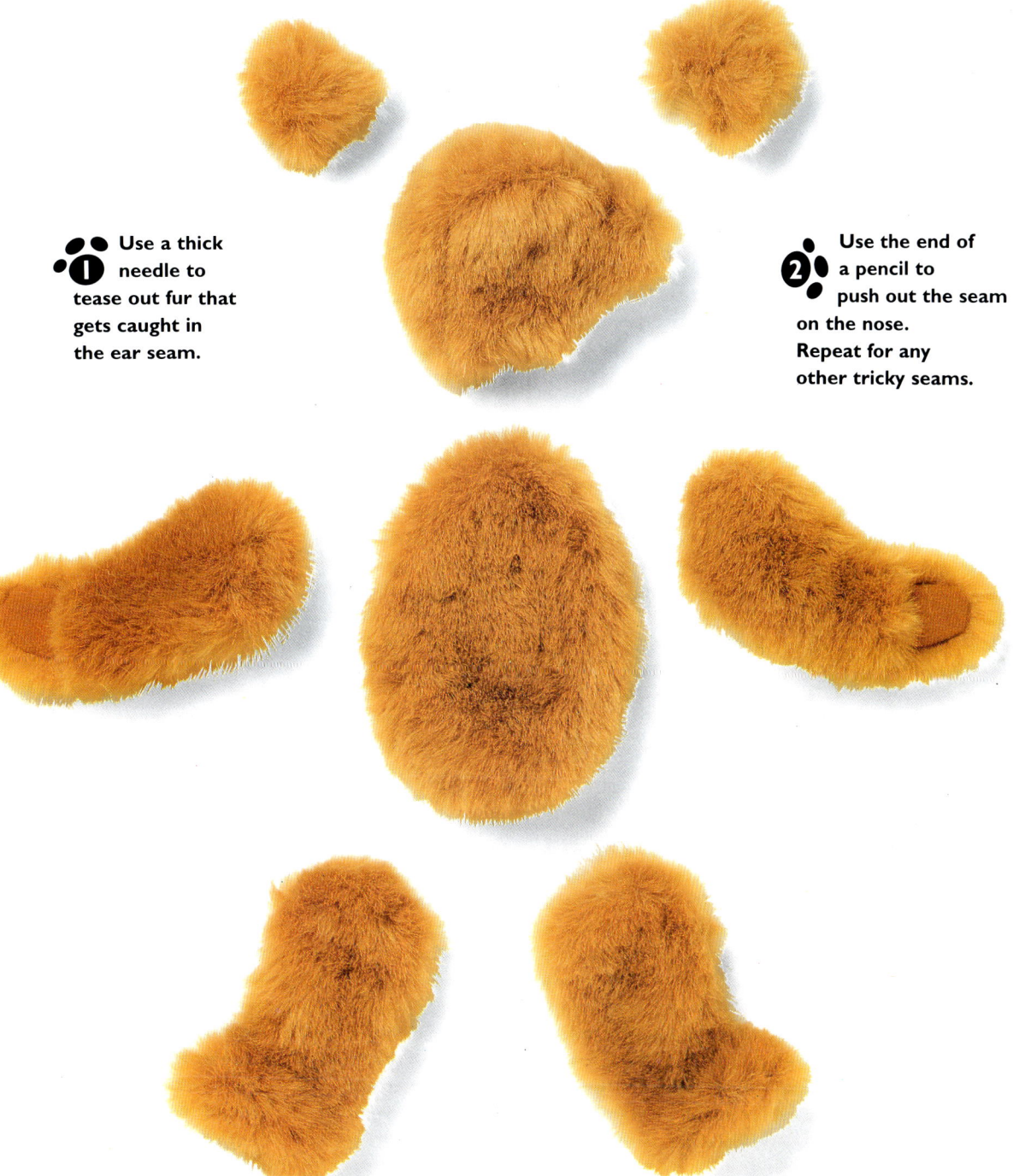

**1** Use a thick needle to tease out fur that gets caught in the ear seam.

**2** Use the end of a pencil to push out the seam on the nose. Repeat for any other tricky seams.

Machine stitch all the pinned pieces with straight stitch and a seam allowance of 6mm (¼in) as before. Make sure there are no pins left in the bear, then turn the pieces right side out. Check all the seams are firm and even.

# Baby Bear

## Stage Seven
# Creating the features

It is a bear's facial features which give it character. Take special care during this part of the procedure.

For safety reasons the eye and nose fasteners must fit very tightly. Securing the fasteners is a fiddly operation which needs to be taken slowly.

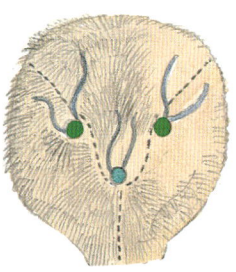

**🐾 1  Eyes and nose:** Using the eye placement points as guidelines, check they are positioned evenly by putting two colour-headed pins on the outside. Adjust the position if necessary. Mark the places with contrasting colour thread. Do the same for the nose, which should be placed centrally on the gusset, immediately next to the point where the gusset seam meets the nose to neck seam.

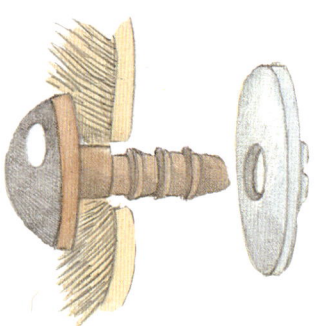

**🐾 3** Press each fastener in as far as it will go by hand; then slip a cotton reel through the shank, and tap lightly with a hammer until the shank shows three ridges.

**🐾 2** Make holes in the two eye points with an awl or thick knitting needle. Slip the shank of each eye through, and secure firmly inside with the safety fastener disc. Then make a hole for the nose, and slip its shank through, securing it with the fastener disc in the inside of the head, as for the eyes. See step 3 for how to secure the eye and nose fasteners.

**🐾 4  Head:** Stuff the head very firmly, making sure you fill the nose well. Thread a needle with strong double thread and run a gathering stitch round the neck edges.

# Baby Bear

🐾 **5** Place half the head joint inside, with the shank sticking out, and pull the gathers tight. Knot and stitch across to secure it in place.

🐾 **6** **Ears:** Find the best position for the ears, holding them in place with pins until you are satisfied they are evenly placed. Do not stuff the ears. Stitch them in place with double strong thread and a curved needle. Take one running stitch from the lower edge of the ear, 6mm (¼in) from the edge, and then one from the head. After two or three stitches pull to close: the stitches will disappear and so will the raw edge of the ear.

🐾 **7** Sew at least twice round the front and back of the ears.

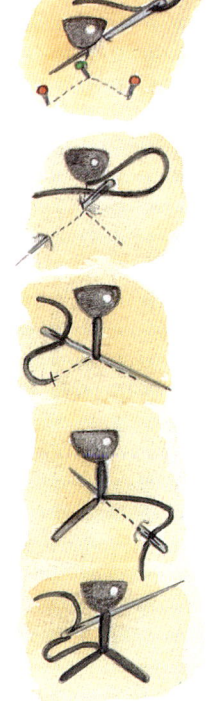

🐾 **8** **Embroidering the mouth:** Mark the desired position with pins and proceed to stitch as shown above, using thread supplied.

🐾 **9** **Trimming the muzzle** Baby Bear's muzzle can be trimmed or you can leave the fur shaggy. Practise on a piece of scrap fur before making any cuts; you need to be confident in your trimming skills before tackling Baby Bear. Using small sharp scissors, trim about 1cm (⅜in) off the length of the fur; ie about half the depth of the pile. Trim from eye level to the sides of the nose and over the mouth area, but leave some fur uncut before reaching the neck.

Before...

...and after

**Baby Bear**

Stage Eight
# Jointing and finishing

This final stage involves jointing the bear and adding the finishing touches. Lay out the bear's limbs with washer discs and fastener discs to ensure you have all the pieces.

# Baby Bear 23

**1.** With the awl, pierce a hole on the top of the body, just by the seam, as indicated in the pattern. Slip through the shank of the head joint. From the inside of the body, and sandwiching the two layers of fur fabric, slip onto the shank the washer disc, and then the fastener disc.

**2.** For safety reasons the fastener discs fit very tightly. Press with your thumbs to push the fastener disc in place as far as possible. Then apply pressure to alternate sides of the fastener disc using your thumbs or tap the rim of the disc with a hammer. Continue until nine ridges can be seen on the shank of the joint.

**3.** For the limb joints, pierce holes with the awl on the inside of the legs and arms as indicated on the pattern. Push the shank joints, from the inside, out through the holes so the shanks protrude. Be careful to make sure that your bear has right and left limbs!

**4.** With the awl, pierce four holes in the body as indicated for the leg and arm joints. Making sure the correct limb goes in the correct hole, push the first leg in, and finish inside the body with the washer disc and fastener disc (as for the head). Repeat for the second leg. Now do the arms, one at a time, closing the joint from the inside of the body, as for the legs.

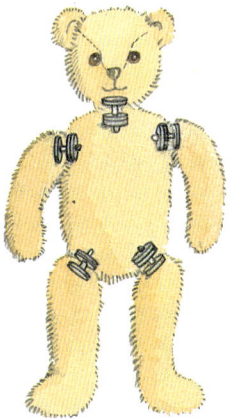

All five joints shown in position. Note the shanks point in towards the body and not towards the limbs.

**5.** Test by moving each joint – it should feel really tight, although it will loosen up a bit with use.

Use a knitting needle or chopstick to stuff the arms and legs first, making sure the filling is pushed right into the ends of paws and toes before putting in the next section of stuffing. Then stuff the body, making sure to fill the shoulder and crotch areas well before stuffing the rest of the body.

**6.** Close the openings by hand, using ladder stitch and strong double thread (as explained for the ears). It is easiest to sew up the limbs first and the body last.

**7.** Using a thick needle, slide the tip under the pile and pull the fibres gently to release any fur trapped in the seams.

Your Baby Bear is now ready and can be dressed (see pages 40-45), or just adorned with a large ribbon bow.

Shank joint

Loose-fitting washer (when fitted, curved edge faces towards shank)

Tight-fitting fastener (when fitted, curved edge faces away from shank)

## YOU WILL NEED

**Short pile mohair**
- 25cm × 150cm (10in × 60in)

**Suedette or velveteen for paws and foot pads**
- 12cm × 15cm (5in × 6in)

**Eyes**
- A pair, 14mm (⁹⁄₁₆in) brown, plastic safety

**Nose**
- Triangular, 18mm (¾in) black plastic safety and a scrap of black or brown gloving leather to cover it

**Joints**
- Five, 35mm (1½in), plastic safety

**Filling**
- 200g (8oz) polyester, high quality

# Mummy Bear

Build on your bear-making experience by creating this delightful, medium-sized, Mummy Bear. You will find a pattern for an easy-to-make dress at the back of the book to give your bear a genuinely individual look.

**For more information** All the basic bear-making skills and stages are spelt out for Baby Bear. So if you find you need more detailed instructions than are given for Mummy Bear, refer back and you will find the help you need on pages 12-23.

# Mummy Bear

## Stage One
# Preparing the pattern

Enlarge the Mummy Bear pattern pieces as described below. Duplicate and reverse pieces as necessary to obtain all the pieces indicated in the list, right.

Check the direction of the pile on the fur fabric, and lay out the pattern pieces in the appropriate direction on the back of it. Pin, then trace round them and transfer all markings. Trace the paws and foot pads onto the back of the pad fabric. Make the nose cover piece on the back of the gloving leather. Cut out all the pieces and lay in "bear shape" to check.

**From fur fabric**

**Ears**
- 4

**Head gusset**
- 1

**Head sides**
- 2, one reversed

**Body front**
- 2, one reversed

**Body back**
- 2, one reversed

**Inner arms**
- 2, one reversed

**Outer arms**
- 2, one reversed

**Legs**
- 4, two reversed

**From suedette**

**Foot pads**
- 2

**Paw pads**
- 2, one reversed

**From gloving leather**

**Nose cover**
- 1

**Enlarging the pattern pieces**
All pattern pieces are shown at half size. Draw a new grid to double the square size shown and carefully redraw the pieces onto it. If you have access to a photocopier set the enlargement to 200% and simply copy the pieces as required.

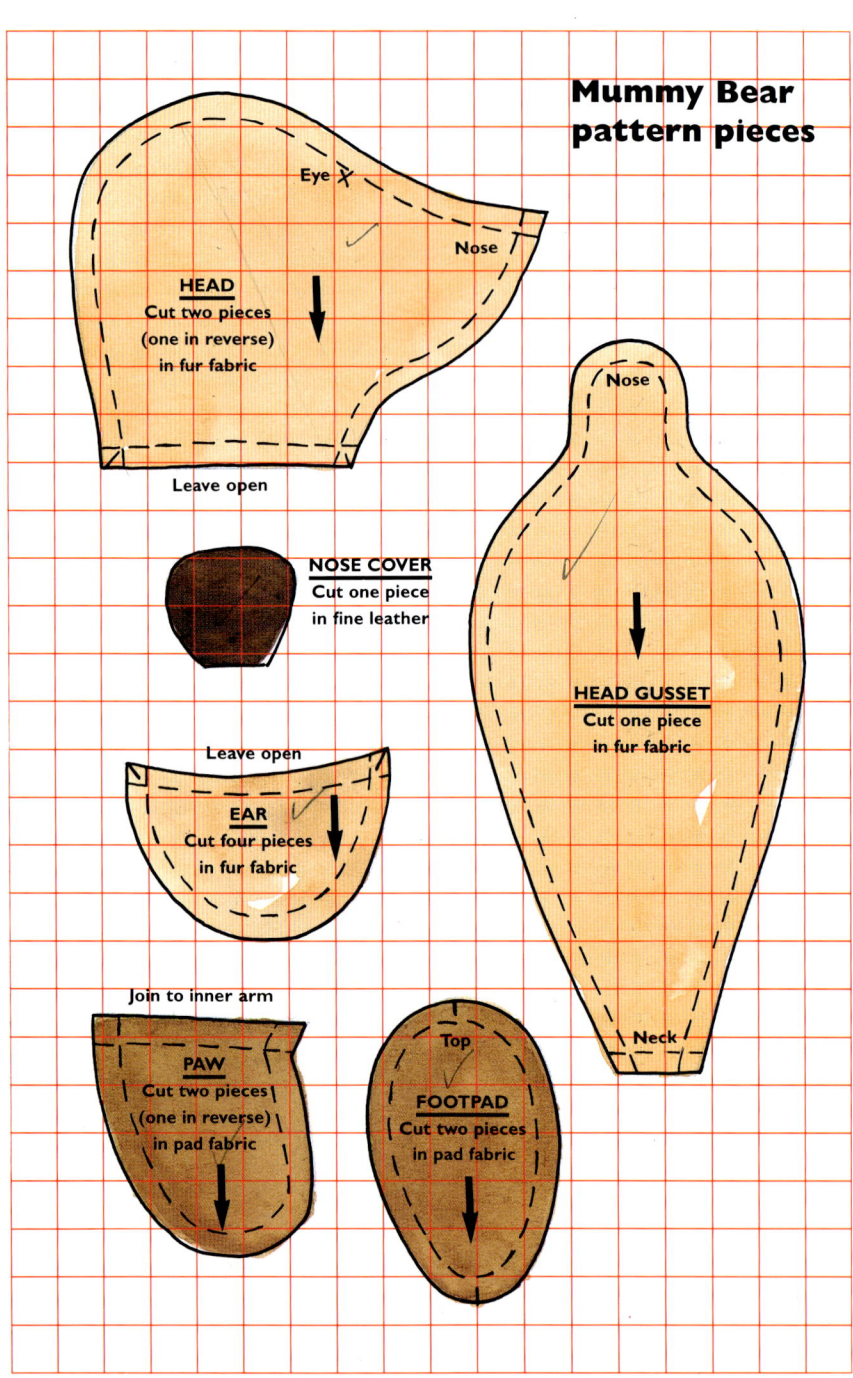

Mummy Bear pattern pieces

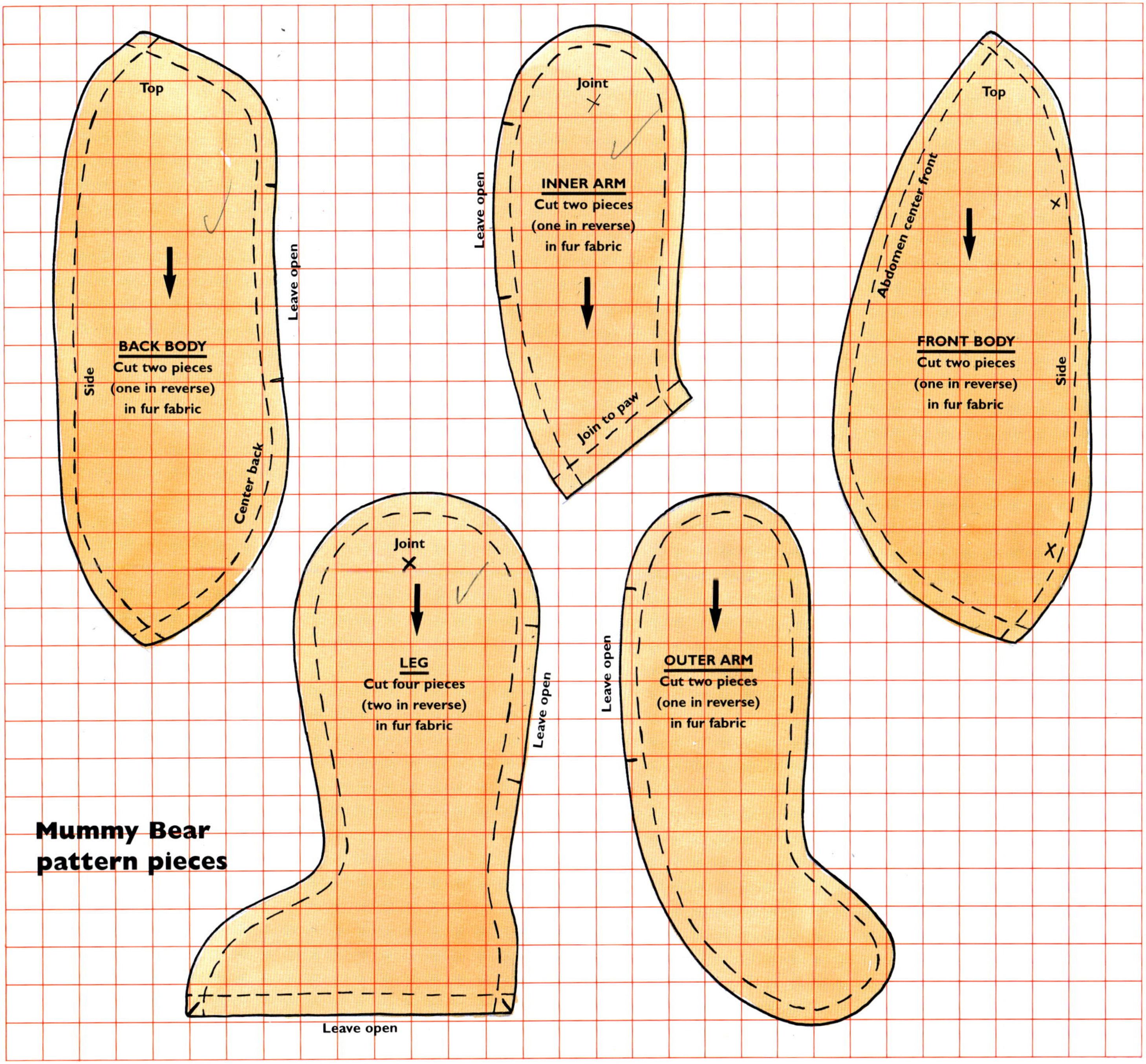

# Mummy Bear

**BACK BODY**
Cut two pieces
(one in reverse)
in fur fabric

*Top · Side · Leave open · Center back*

**INNER ARM**
Cut two pieces
(one in reverse)
in fur fabric

*Joint · Leave open · Join to paw*

**FRONT BODY**
Cut two pieces
(one in reverse)
in fur fabric

*Top · Abdomen center front · Side*

**LEG**
Cut four pieces
(two in reverse)
in fur fabric

*Joint · Leave open · Leave open*

**OUTER ARM**
Cut two pieces
(one in reverse)
in fur fabric

*Leave open*

**Mummy Bear pattern pieces**

# Mummy Bear

## Stage Two
# Pinning and sewing

Putting right sides together, pin and then machine stitch the pieces shown on this page.

**1.** Pin and stitch the two ears, two pieces together at a time, around the long curved side.

**2.** Pin and stitch the side heads together, from nose to neck only.

**3.** Pin and stitch the two back bodies to each other, along the centre back seam only, being careful to leave an opening in the centre of the seam as indicated.

**4.** Pin and stitch the legs, two together at a time, leaving two openings in each leg: one to fit the foot pad, and one on the back to turn the legs right side out.

**5.** Pin and stitch each suedette paw to the corresponding inner arm.

**6.** Pin and stitch the two front bodies to each other, along the centre (tummy) seam only.

**Stage Three**
# Joining the pieces

**Mummy Bear**

1. Join the gusset to the head sides. Start at the centre of the nose end, and leave a small gap in the very centre to insert the nose. Pin and tack from the centre along one side up to the point where the gusset widens. Stop, go back to the centre, and do the other side. Then pin and tack the remainder of the two seams. Now stitch one side at a time, working from the centre of the nose towards the neck edge. (For more details, see page 18, step 1.)

2. Join right sides together. Pin and stitch the inner arms to the outer arms, all around, leaving an opening on the side.

3. Join right sides together. Pin and stitch the completed front body to the completed back body. Open the pieces up, and join them all around, leaving only a tiny 3mm (1/8in) gap at the very top for the head joint, where all seams meet. The bear will be turned right side out through the opening in the back seam.

4. Join right sides together. Pin and tack the foot pads to the lower leg openings, matching front and back of pads to the relevant seams in each leg. Stitch in place.

Join right sides together, pin and machine stitch as shown on this page.

## Mummy Bear

# Stage Four
# Eyes, nose and mouth

Turn all the pieces right side out, and proceed to create the face features (for more details, see pages 20-21).

**2** Check that the markings for the eyes are even, and fit the eyes and the nose on the bear using the safety fixings. Stuff the head very firmly. Run a gathering stitch around the neck opening, fit one half of a 35mm (1½in) joint inside, with the shank sticking out, pull the gathers and close. Stitch the ears in place and embroider the mouth.

**1** Take the gloving leather nose cover piece, and run a small gathering stitch, using doubled strong thread, all around it. Place the plastic nose inside it, with the shank sticking out. (See detail, above.) Pull the gathers firmly and knot (see detail, below). Do some stitches across to secure and flatten the gathers. Knot again and finish off neatly.

Stage Five

# Jointing and finishing

**Mummy Bear**

**1.** Slip the shank of the head joint through the gap left at the top of the body and close the joint tightly from the inside, using the disc and the washer.

**2.** Fit two other 35mm (1½in) half-joints inside the legs (mirror image, so the bear has a left and a right side!) and the two remaining half-joints inside the inner arms. Leave the shanks protruding outside.

Assemble the bear by fitting the joints in the limbs and joining them as shown on page 23.

**3.** Check that the markings for joining the limbs to the body are evenly placed. Attach the arms and legs to the body, and close the joints from the inside. Ensure the joints are tightly fitted; for more details, see page 23, step 2. Stuff the limbs first, then the body. Close all openings with ladder stitch. Complete Mummy Bear with clothes or a bow.

## YOU WILL NEED

**Long pile "distressed" mohair**
• 50cm × 70cm (20in × 28in)

**Ultrasuede, suedette or thick 100% wool felt for paws and foot pads**
• 12cm × 16cm (5in × 6in)

**Eyes**
• A pair, 14mm (9/16in) glass with wire loops. Alternatively, 16mm (5/8in) brown, plastic safety

**Nose**
• Embroidered with brown or black perlé embroidery thread

**Joints**
• Five 50mm (2in) hardboard and split pin joints. Alternatively, five 45mm (1¾in) plastic safety joints

**Filling**
• 300g (12oz) polyester, high quality

# Daddy Bear

If you have made **Mummy Bear** and **Baby Bear**, you will have no problems in creating your very own 'antique' collectors' bear – complete with the traditional long arms, embroidered claws, long snout and humped back. If you use safety eyes and joints, this bear will still be suitable as a toy.

**For more information** All the basic bear-making skills and stages are spelt out for Baby Bear. So if you find you need more detailed instructions than are given for Daddy Bear, refer back and you will find the help you need on pages 12-23.

# Daddy Bear

## Stage One
# Preparing the pattern

Enlarge the Daddy Bear pattern pieces as described below. Duplicate and reverse pieces as necessary, to obtain all the pieces indicated in the list, right.

Check best direction of the pile, then lay out the pattern pieces in the appropriate direction on the back of the fur fabric. Trace round them and transfer all markings. Mark paws and foot pads on the back of the pad fabric. Cut out and lay all the pieces in a "bear shape" to check.

**From fur fabric**

Ears
- 4

Head gusset
- 1

Head sides
- 2, one reversed

Body
- 2, one reversed

Arms
- 2, one reversed

Legs
- 2, one reversed

**From pad fabric**

Foot pads
- 2

Paw pads
- 2, one reversed

**Enlarging the pattern pieces**
All pattern pieces are shown at half size. Draw a new grid to double the square size shown and carefully redraw the pieces onto it. If you have access to a photocopier set the enlargement to 200% and simply copy the pieces as required.

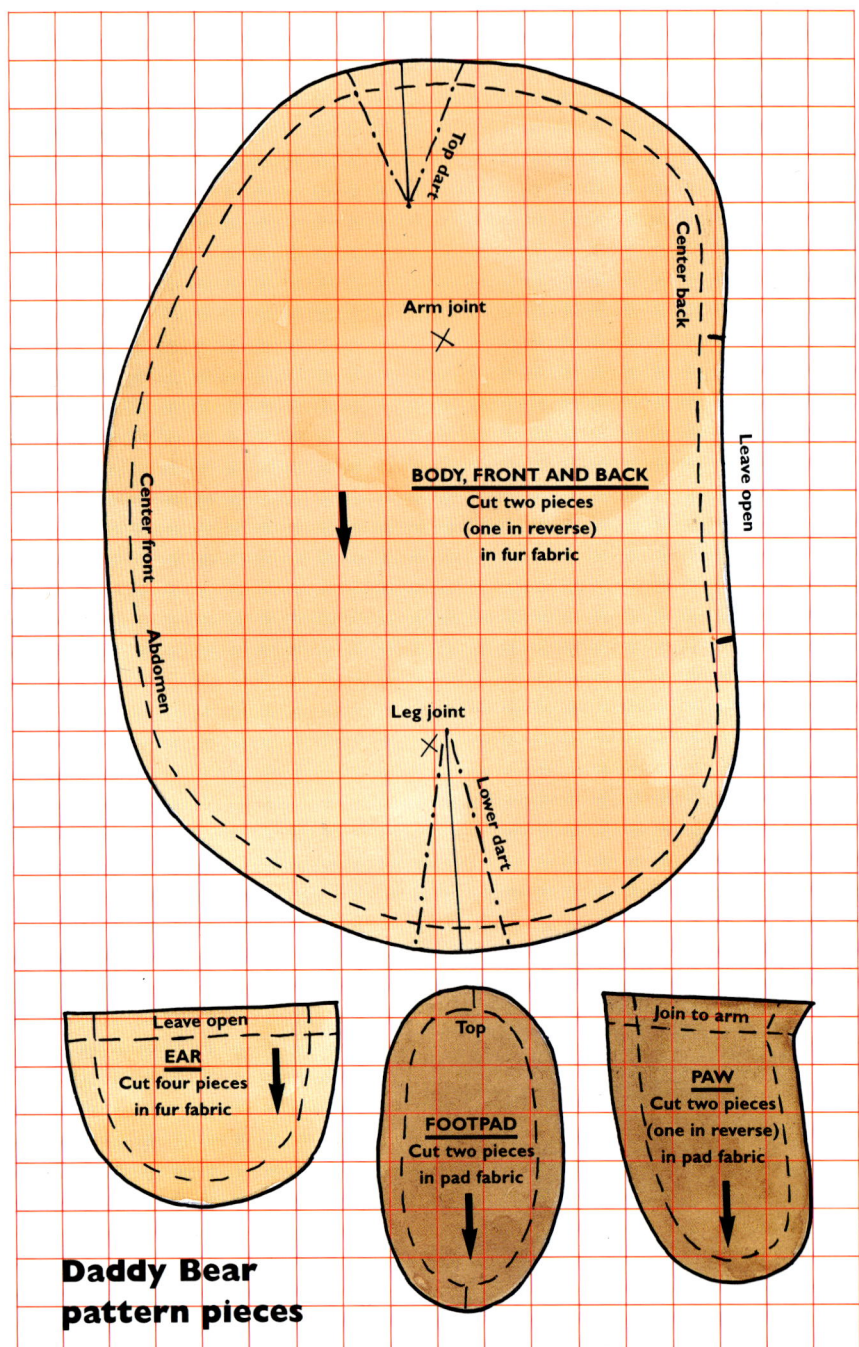

**Daddy Bear pattern pieces**

# Daddy Bear

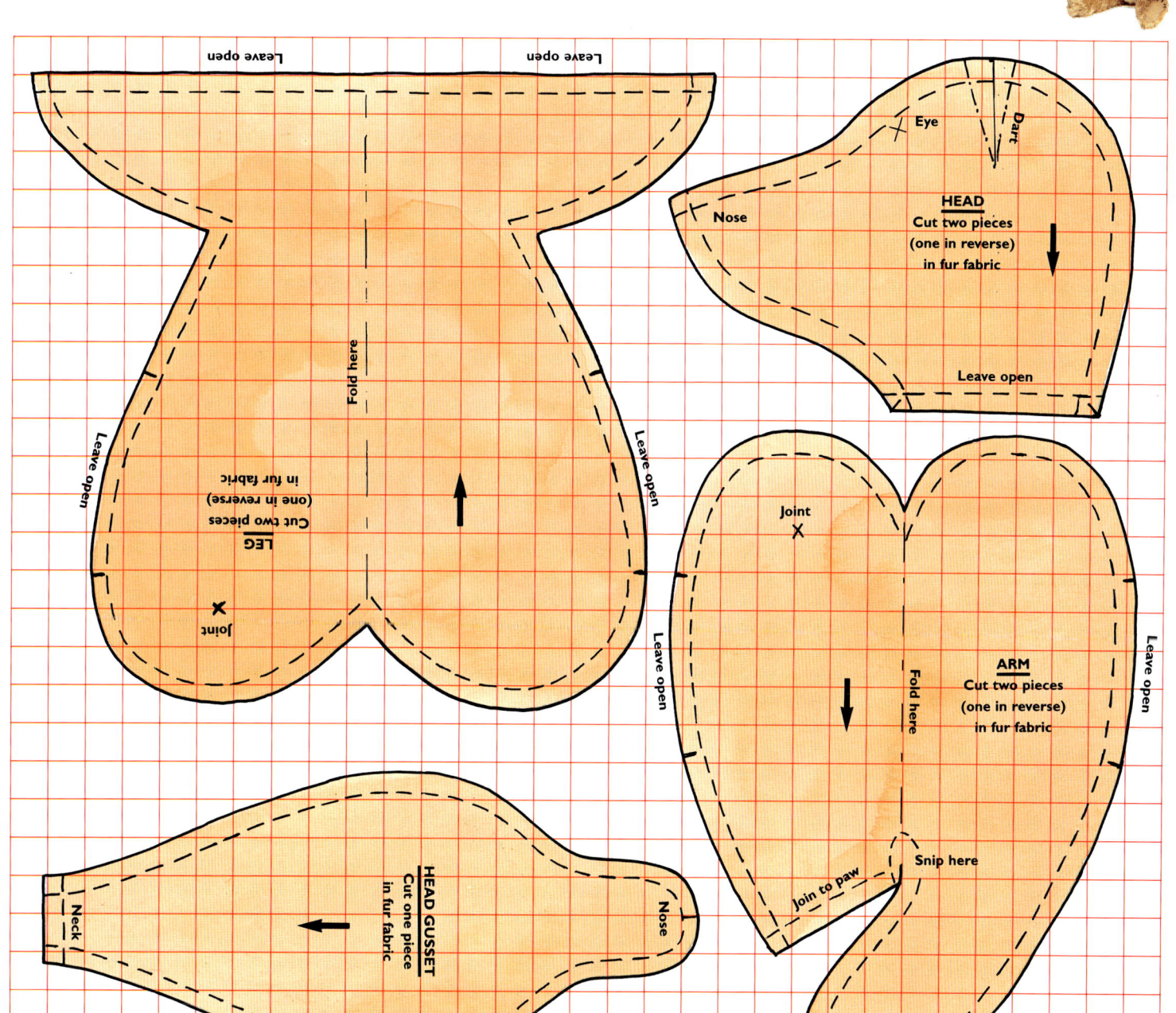

Daddy Bear pattern pieces

# Daddy Bear

## Stage Two
# Pinning and sewing

Right sides together, pin and machine stitch the pieces shown on this page.

**1.** Pin and stitch the darts in the two side head pieces, then pin and stitch the two sides together from nose to neck only.

**2.** Pin and stitch the two ears, around the long curved side.

**5.** Pin and stitch the paws to the inner side of arms. These need careful positioning – double check the photograph (below) before you sew.

**3.** Pin and stitch the body darts (two on each side of the body).

**4.** Pin and stitch the legs: fold over and leave two openings, one to fit foot pads and one to turn the legs right side out.

## Stage Three
# Joining the pieces

**Daddy Bear** 37

Right sides together, pin and machine stitch the pieces as shown on this page.

1. Pin and stitch the gusset to the head sides, starting at the nose end.

2. Pin, tack and stitch the nose area first, then do the rest, working from the nose towards the neck edge, one side at a time.

3. Fold over the arms, pin and stitch, leaving an opening on the side for turning right side out. The paw should match the arm.

4. Pin and stitch the foot pads to the lower leg openings, matching the front of each pad to the front leg seam.

5. Pin and stitch the body, all around, leaving an opening at the back for turning.

6. Turn all the pieces right side out.

# Daddy Bear

## Stage Four
# Jointing and finishing

This last stage is where you can give your bear its own special, unique expression – happy, thoughtful, alert, mischievous.

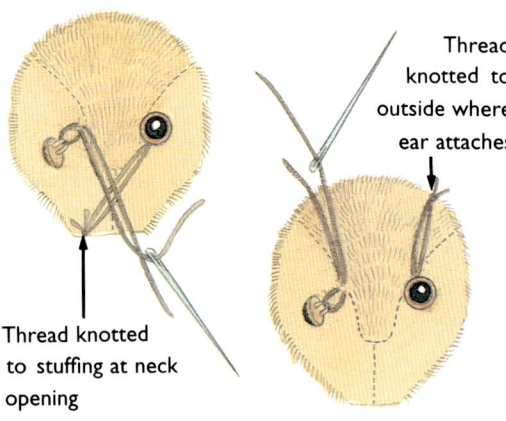

Thread knotted to stuffing at neck opening

Thread knotted to outside where ear attaches

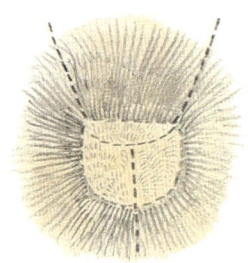

🐾 **1** If you are using safety plastic eyes, fit them on your bear now, as shown on page 20. Stuff the head very firmly. If you are using glass eyes, stitch them in place on the stuffed head. Use an extra-long needle and double-strong thread, taking the ends of the thread out either down through the neck or up into the ear position, so that knots can be hidden. By pulling the thread tight (especially if it is done across from opposite sides of the neck), an indentation will result, and a kind of "soft sculpture" effect can be obtained.

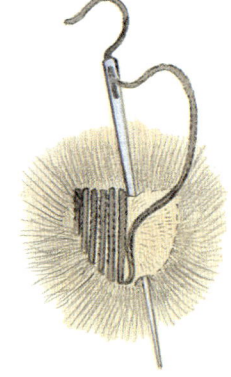

🐾 **2** Either before or after embroidering the nose, decide if you want to cut the hair on the muzzle or not. If you do, use small pointed scissors and pull the pile up so it is cut evenly. You can trim just the top nose area, leaving long hair at the side, or leave the muzzle completely uncut except for the area where the nose will be embroidered. This must be shaven, so hairs do not show through the threads. Alternatively you can shave it almost to the backing (as seen on many old bears), or leave it ⅛in (3mm) long.

🐾 **3** Embroider the nose, using double "perlé" thread or darning wool. Decide on the shape and outline it with stitches. If you haven't trimmed the whole muzzle, cut the fur short in the enclosed area. Fill with parallel stitches, going back and forth several times until it is well covered.

# Daddy Bear 39

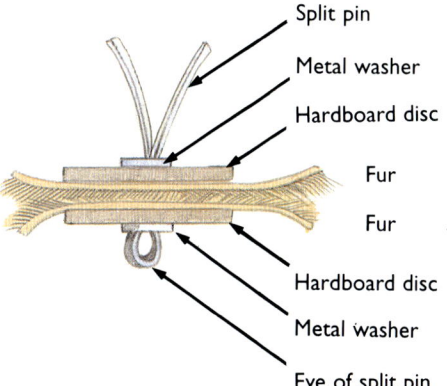

- Split pin
- Metal washer
- Hardboard disc
- Fur
- Fur
- Hardboard disc
- Metal washer
- Eye of split pin

**4.** Stitch the mouth thinking carefully what expression you want your bear to have. Sew the ears in place.

**5.** Separate the two halves of a hardboard joint; do not lose the small metal washer. Run a gathering stitch round the neck opening and fit the half of the joint with a washer, disc and split pin, inside. Pull the gathers and close firmly. (If you are using plastic joints see page 23.)

**6.** Pierce a hole on the top of the body, right next to the seam. Slip the split pin of the head joint through the hole and slip the other disc and washer through the split pin. You will need to secure this tightly in place by making a crown joint.

**7.** For a crown joint each side of the split pin has to be twisted with a pair of long-nose pliers so that it rests on the small metal washer, and holds the joint very tightly. Follow the stages shown in the diagrams (right).

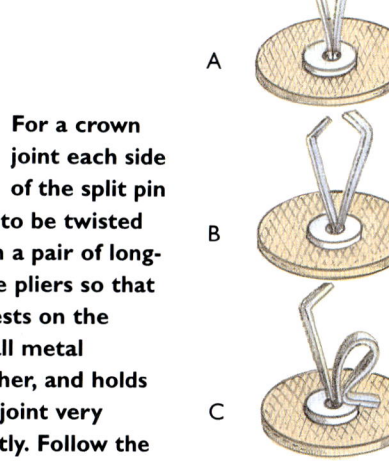

A
B
C
D

**8.** Fit the other half-joints inside the legs and the inner arms. Leave split pins protruding outside. Check that the jointing points are even, and attach the arms and legs to the body, and close the joints from the inside. Stuff the limbs first, the body afterwards. Close all openings with ladder stitch.

**9.** You can create claws, four to each paw and pad, using a length of double perlé thread and a long needle. Finish Daddy Bear with a waistcoat, a tie, a scarf or simply a ribbon and bow.

# Bear Wear

Teddy Bears do not need to wear clothes – their fur keeps them warm! But it does make a bear extra special and individual if you take a little time to give it a few finishing touches. A simple ribbon bow may suit your bear best – or maybe he deserves more!

Our three bears can be dressed with clothes made from the patterns provided here: a small waistcoat for Baby Bear, and a larger version for Daddy Bear; a simple dress for Mummy Bear, and a smaller size for a she-Baby Bear. Choose fabrics carefully, and add ribbons, lace, silk flowers and other little accessories if appropriate.

# Bear Wear

# Bear waistcoats

Most fabrics are suitable for making the waistcoats: cotton, polyester, wool, velvet or even silk. The lining can be made in the same fabric if you use cotton or polyester, but a different, thinner type of lining is recommended for thicker materials such as wool or velvet.

**Baby Bear's waistcoat:**
- 15cm × 35cm (6in × 14in) of fabric for outside
- 15cm × 35cm (6in × 14in) of fabric for lining
- 2 small buttons plus press studs if you don't want to make buttonholes; sewing thread to match fabric

**Daddy Bear's waistcoat:**
- 23cm × 54cm (9in × 21in) of fabric for outside
- 23cm × 54cm (9in × 21in) of fabric for lining
- 3 small buttons plus press studs if you don't want to make buttonholes; sewing thread to match fabric

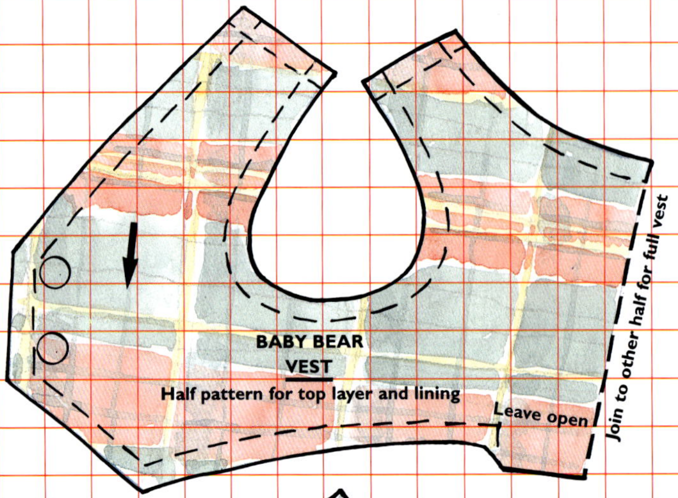

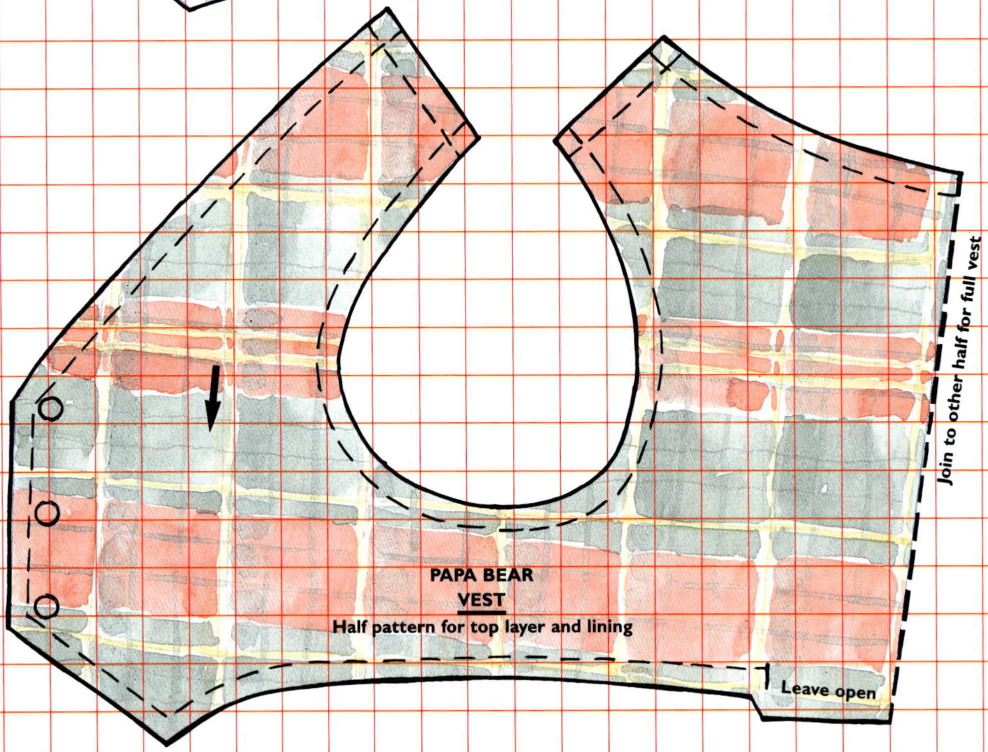

**Enlarging the pattern pieces**
All pattern pieces are shown at half size. Draw a new grid to double the square size shown and carefully redraw the pieces onto it. If you have access to a photocopier set the enlargement to 200% and simply copy the pieces as required.

**BABY BEAR VEST**
Half pattern for top layer and lining
Leave open
Join to other half for full vest

**PAPA BEAR VEST**
Half pattern for top layer and lining
Leave open
Join to other half for full vest

# Bear Wear

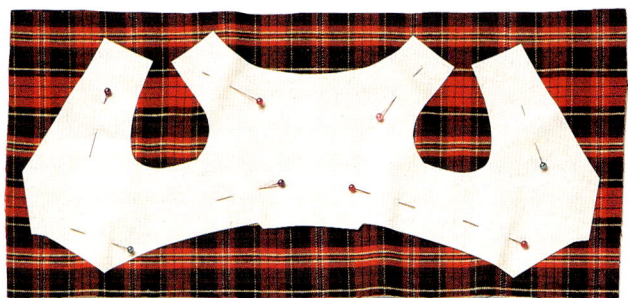

🐾 **1** Following the instructions for enlarging the pattern pieces (see left), trace or photocopy the pattern in the desired size twice. Cut the paper pieces out and join with sticky tape to make a one-piece waistcoat pattern. Place the waistcoat fabric and the lining right sides together, and put the prepared pattern on top. Pin together or hold in place. Mark the waistcoat shape on the fabric with the pencil or dressmakers' chalk.

🐾 **2** Remove the paper pattern but keep the two pieces of fabric pinned together so they do not slip while they are being stitched. *Do not cut yet.* Prepare the sewing machine for your choice of fabric, then stitch all around 6mm (¼in) *inside* the marked lines. Leave an opening in the centre of the lower back seam as indicated. Now cut the waistcoat out following the marked lines. Clip curved seams and trim corners.

🐾 **3** Turn right side out, carefully pushing out corners and seams with a knitting needle from the inside. Press flat, and close the opening with ladder stitch.

🐾 **4** Try the waistcoat on your bear. Pin the shoulder seams together by overlapping the front over the back. Mark the position of the buttons (and buttonholes, if you are going to make them). Take the waistcoat off the bear, and machine or hand-stitch the shoulder seams. Stitch the buttons in place, either making buttonholes to match, or stitching press studs under the buttons to close the waistcoat. A bow tie in matching or contrasting ribbon is a delightful extra.

# Bear Wear

# Bear dresses

This is a very simple dress made of fabric rectangles. However you can achieve very different effects by varying the fabrics and accessories you choose. Simple cotton prints make for a homely, country bear, while velvet and brocade create a more sophisticated teddy!

Appropriate accessories and trims – shawls, ribbon, lace, flowers or beads – also give very different results. You can rearrange the position of the straps (making them wider or narrower) or lengthen or shorten the skirt to suit your bear's personality.
No patterns are necessary for these dresses. Use a ruler to measure rectangles and cut them from the fabric; measurements are given above.

## You will need

### Baby Bear's dress

- 23cm × 90cm (9in × 36in) of fabric
- Button, press stud or piece of Velcro
- Sewing thread to match fabric

### Mummy Bear's dress

- 30cm × 90cm (12in × 36in) of fabric
- Button, press stud or piece of Velcro
- Sewing thread to match fabric

**Skirt**

**Waistband**

**Wide straps**

**For Baby Bear**
Skirt
- 12cm × 60cm (5in × 24in)

Waistband
- 8cm × 40cm (3in × 15in)

Wide straps
- two, each 8cm × 20cm (3in × 8in)

**For Mummy Bear**
Skirt
- 20cm × 66cm (8in × 26in)

Waistband
- 8cm × 38cm (3in × 15in)

Wide straps
- two, each 10cm × 25cm (4in × 10in)

**1** Fold the skirt rectangle in half, right sides together. Matching the short sides, pin and stitch to half way up the join. Press the seam open, turning in the remaining half of the seam to make a hem. Stitch that hem in place.

Now make a bottom hem by turning up the lower edge (where the short edges are joined together) 10mm (⅜in) twice. Pin and machine stitch.

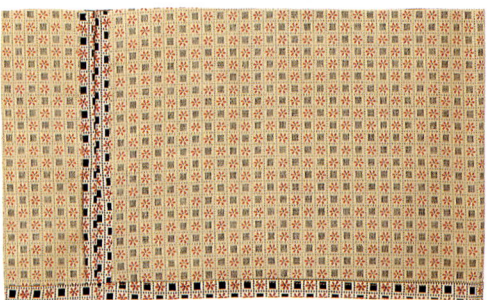

# Bear Wear 45

**2.** Gather the top edge by running two lines of stitching with a long stitch size along the top edge of the skirt, 6mm (¼in) and 10mm (⅜in) from the edge. Pull the gathers from both ends until the skirt fits your bear's waist. Knot the thread ends and even out the gathers.

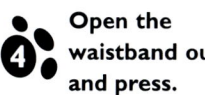 **4.** Open the waistband out and press. Turn in 6mm (¼in) along the other long edge of the waistband, and pin it, but do not stitch yet. Fold inwards and pin the short edges to neaten, cutting off any surplus beyond 12mm (½in). Now fold the waistband over, wrong sides together, and pin the turned-in narrow hem to the back of the skirt waist. Top-stitch by machine or hem stitch by hand in place. Do not forget to stitch the two short edges as well. Put a button and buttonhole or press stud or sew on Velcro to close the waistband.

**3.** Right sides together, pin one of the long edges of the waistband to the gathered edge of the skirt, allowing the ends of the waistband to stick out at each end. Machine stitch in place.

 **5.** Narrow hem the long edges of the straps. Put the skirt on the bear and lay the straps in place, moving them until you have the best position. Pin them to the waistband at the front and back, making sure the closure at the back is left free. Carefully remove the dress from the bear and stitch the straps in place, either by hand on the inside or by machine using top stitching on to the waistband.

# Bears! Bears! Bears!

The bears on these two pages were made using the patterns featured in this book. Choice of fur, stuffing and accessories make each bear unique.

**Old Brown Grizzly** (left) A large bear in smart striped waistcoat. With all the safety features, he is perfect as a child's best friend. (Daddy bear pattern.) **Hug-me Ted** (below left) Irresistible teddy in baby-soft synthetic fur fabric with velvet pads, safety eyes and nose – a cuddly companion to a small child. (Baby Bear pattern.) **A Friend For Life** (below right) Long straight ivory mohair, embroidered nose, glass eyes, luxurious leather pads – a classic bear to cherish for ever. (Baby Bear pattern.)

**Growling Bear** (below) Made in distressed mohair, this delightful antique bear has a growler in his tummy.

**Sleek Bear** (left) Short, dark mohair creates a leaner looking bear in need of lots of tender loving care. Child-safe plastic eyes and nose are used. (Baby Bear pattern.)

**Grandpa Bear** (right) For collectors, this bear has extra long-pile mohair fur and is filled with wood wool. His eyes and ears are placed higher on his head to give him an older and wiser appearance. (Daddy Bear pattern.)

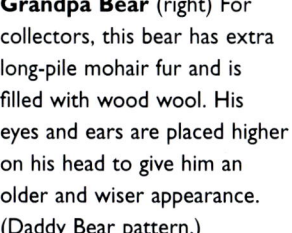
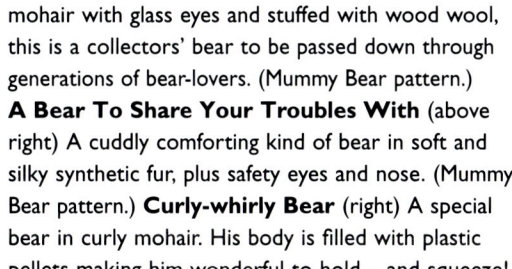

**Heirloom Teddy Bear** (above left) In "tipped" mohair with glass eyes and stuffed with wood wool, this is a collectors' bear to be passed down through generations of bear-lovers. (Mummy Bear pattern.)
**A Bear To Share Your Troubles With** (above right) A cuddly comforting kind of bear in soft and silky synthetic fur, plus safety eyes and nose. (Mummy Bear pattern.) **Curly-whirly Bear** (right) A special bear in curly mohair. His body is filled with plastic pellets making him wonderful to hold – and squeeze! (Baby Bear pattern; not suitable for children.)

## Useful contacts
Suppliers of fur, pad fabrics, eyes, noses, joints, fillings, felts etc.

## United Kingdom
**Margaret & Gerry Grey's Teddy Shop**
The Old Bakery Gallery,
38 Cambridge St,
Wellingborough,
Northampton NN8 1DW.
Tel: (0933) 229191
Fax: (0933) 272466

**Oakley Fabrics**
8 May St, Luton LU1 3QY.
Tel: (0582) 424828
Fax: (0582) 455274

## Australia & New Zealand
**Gerry's**
30 John St, Rosewood,
QLD 4340.
(Tel/Fax 074 64 1479

**Dee Glossop Teddy Bears and Accessories**
86 Model Farms Road,
Winston Hills 2154.
Tel/Fax: 6861682

**Lavals Distributors**
Unit 10/3-5 Tooranga Ave,
Edwardstown, SA 5039.

**Bartfield Textiles Pty Ltd**
576 Glenhuntley Road,
Elsternwick VIC 3185.
Tel: (03) 523 6641

**Furtex**
Heath Furs & Textiles Ltd,
28 Tobin Street, Pukekohe,
New Zealand.
Tel: (09) 238 3402

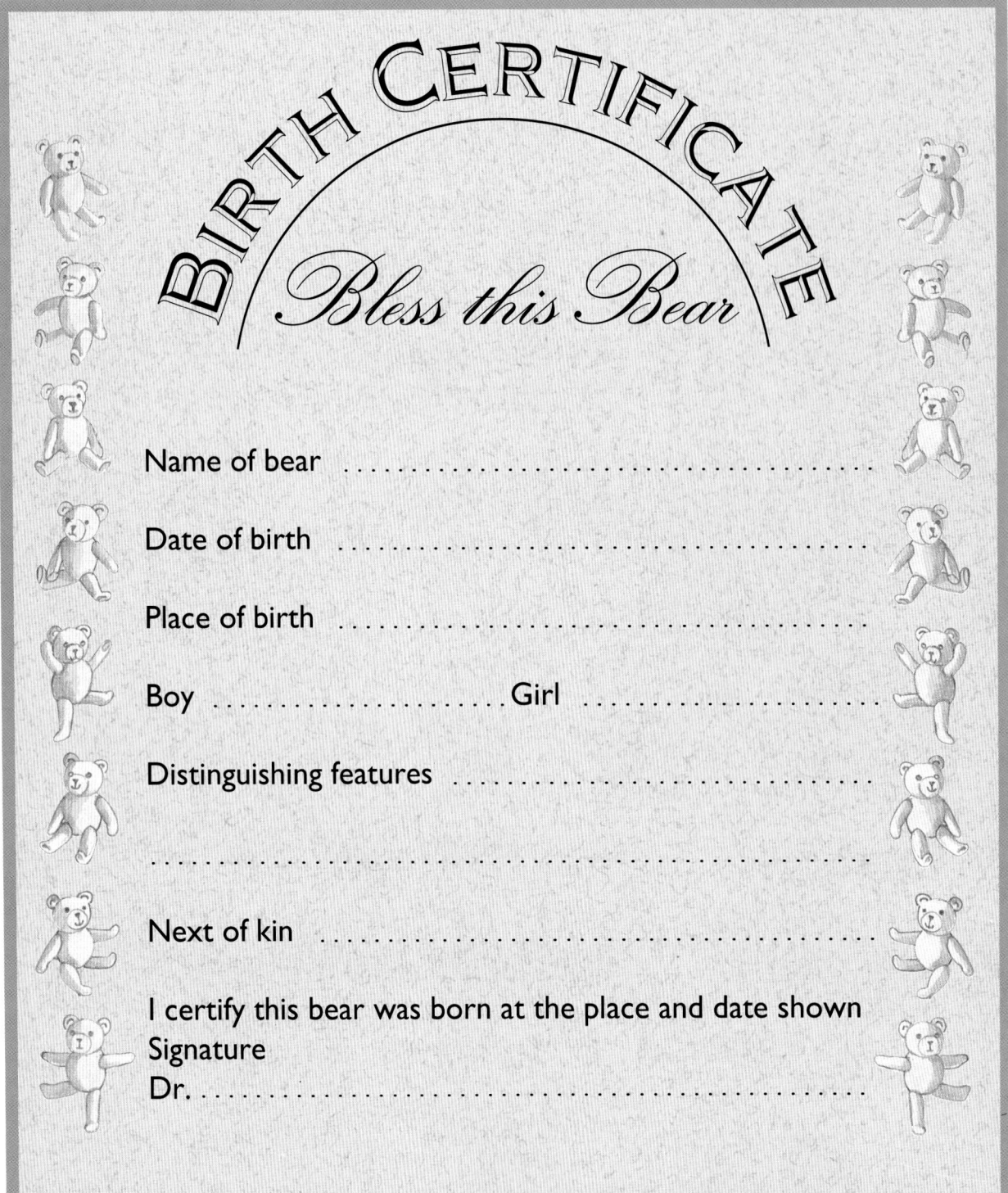